Victorian Life
Clothes

Liz Gogerly

WAYLAND

First published in 2008 by Wayland

Copyright © Wayland 2008
This paperback edition published in 2012 by Wayland
Wayland
338 Euston Road
London NW1 3BH

Wayland Australia
Level 17/207 Kent Street
Sydney, NSW 2000

Editor: Katie Powell
Designer: Jane Hawkins
Design concept: Paul Cherrill

British Library Cataloguing in Publication Data

Gogerly, Liz
   Clothes. - (Victorian life)
   1. Clothing and dress - Great Britain - History - 19th
century - Juvenile literature 2. Great Britain - Social
life and customs - 19th century - Juvenile literature
   I. Title
   391'.00941'09034

ISBN 978 0 7502 6876 9

Printed in China

Picture acknowledgements:
Bettmann/Corbis: 9TR, 21, 28B; Bridgeman Art Library/Sir John Everett;
Millais/Getty Images: 18; Mary Evans Picture Library: 3, 10, 11, 13, 16, 20,
22CL, 26, 28C, 30; Getty Images/Hulton Archive: 7, 15B, 19, 25B; JFB/Art Archive:
24; Collection Kharbine-Tapabor, Paris, France/Bridgeman Art Library, London:
15T; Lake County Museum/Corbis: 17; London Stereoscopic Company/Hulton
Archive/Getty Images: Cover – main image, 12; John Meek/Art Archive: 27;
Private Collection/Bridgeman Art Library, London: 23; Wayland Archive: Cover
BR, 4, 5, 6, 8, 9TL, 14, 22BC, 25T, 28T

With thanks to www.victorianlondon.org

Wayland is a division of Hachette Children's Books,
an Hachette UK company
www.hachette.co.uk

Contents

Words in **bold** can be found
in the glossary.

The Victorians

The Victorians lived during Queen's Victoria rule of Britain from 1837 to 1901 – longer than any other British king or queen. During that time there were huge changes in the way people lived and dressed.

⬆ People dancing and enjoying themselves at a fair on Hampstead Heath in London, 1880.

The simple life

At the beginning of the Victorian era most people lived in the countryside. The main form of transport was the horse. Middle class and lower class people made their own clothes. Richer people wore clothes made for them by servants or dressmakers. Life was simple for everyone but it was all about to change.

Industrial power

By 1901, most people lived in towns and cities, where there was more work, in factories for example. New means of transport, such as the railway, had also made travelling easier. The population had grown from 16 million to 37 million people and this meant there was greater demand for everything, including food, housing and clothes.

Fortunately, the Victorians were great inventors. Machines took the place of people power and factories poured out goods. Industry boomed during the **Industrial Revolution** and Britain was the most powerful and richest nation in the world.

The Victorian wardrobe

When Queen Victoria came to the throne in 1837, the kind of clothes that people wore in Britain were quite **formal**. Men wore jackets, shirts and trousers. Women wore dresses or gowns. Children dressed like adults. Today we still wear the same basic types of clothes worn by the Victorians, but the fashions and fabrics have come a long way since then. However, it is the Victorians who invented new machines that meant faster and cheaper clothes production for us today.

As a young woman Queen Victoria wore colourful dresses. As an older woman she always dressed in black.

Queen Victoria, 1819–1901

In 1837, Britain welcomed Queen Victoria to the throne. The Queen was just eighteen and ruled Britain for the next 64 years. The clothes and jewellery she wore often influenced the fashions of the day. When her husband Prince Albert died in 1861, Queen Victoria went into deep mourning (grieving). She wore black clothes and had a piece of jewellery made from Albert's hair. This kind of jewellery became fashionable in Britain after Prince Albert's death.

Industry and empire

Britain was known as 'the workshop of the world' in Victorian times. The country had a large empire across the globe. **Colonies,** such as India, brought new opportunities for trade, extending Britain's power.

The textile industry

In the early 1800s, the first **power looms** were being used. These were large weaving machines that were powered by steam. In 1837, Britain was the top cotton manufacturer in the world. Nearly 30 per cent of the population worked in the industry. Cheaper cotton meant that most people wore cotton clothes. However, the downside to the industry was the appalling working conditions. People worked long hours for low pay.

A day in the life of...

...a female shirt worker from a factory in London, 1849–1850:

'I often work in the summer time from four in the morning to nine or ten at night – as long as I can see ... But when there's a press of business, I work earlier and later. I often gets up at two and three in the morning, and carries on till the evening of the following day, merely lying down in my clothes to take a nap of five or ten minutes.'

From a letter by Henry Mayhew, published in *The Morning Chronicle*, 1849.

These women worked long hours in a cotton mill. Victorian factory workers usually wore clothes made from coarsely woven wool or cotton cloth.

Isaac Singer's sewing machine was the first successful mass-produced machine. This model was powered by turning the handle at the side by hand.

The girl is using an 'updated' Singer sewing machine. It uses a foot **treadle** to move the needle up and down.

THE FIRST LESSON ON THE SINGER Sewing Machine

THE NEW IMPROVED SINGER.
EASY TO USE — EASY TO LEARN — EASY TO BUY.

The British Empire

The **British Empire** was the largest empire in history. During Queen Victoria's **reign** the empire grew. Large chunks of Africa, Asia and Japan were **acquired**. This meant Britain had even more access to **raw materials** such as coal or cotton from all over the world. It also meant that Britain dominated trade to these areas. People throughout the world bought British cloth and clothes.

Who made fashion?

Britain was the world's first superpower and leading industrial power – producing more than half the world's iron, coal and cotton. What people wore in Britain influenced fashion throughout the world.

The Great Exhibition

Queen Victoria's husband, Prince Albert, was interested in science and industry. He hosted the Great Exhibition of 1851. It showcased all the marvellous inventions of the age, including the sewing machine, which had been invented by the American, Isaac Singer in 1846.

⬆ The Great Exhibition of 1851 was open for six months. Visitors could get a glimpse of fabrics, clothing and jewels from all over the world.

Over 6 million people came to London to see the exhibition held at the Crystal Palace in Hyde Park. Amongst the **exhibits** were examples of clothing. On display were fine fabrics that had been **manufactured** in Britain. The exhibition showed that Britain lead the way in the textile and clothing industries.

Famous faces

In Victorian times clothes stayed fashionable for much longer than they do today. Some items were popular for up to ten years. But just like modern times, famous people influenced the fashions of the age. The Scottish patterned fabric, tartan, became fashionable because Queen Victoria liked it.

The first cardigan

During the **Crimean War** (1853–1856) the Seventh Earl of Cardigan wore a kind of knitted **military** style jacket. After the war the style caught on in Britain. The jacket was called a cardigan and it is still popular today.

The nurse Florence Nightingale was one of the first Victorian women to stop wearing the crinoline dress (see page 12). Many women soon followed her example.

Charles Macintosh, 1766–1843

The Scottish inventor Charles Macintosh discovered how to lay rubber onto woven woollen cloth by accident. He was working on another project when he found a way of dissolving rubber. The rubber could then be stuck to fabric to make it waterproof. This new material was called 'Mackintosh'. The first 'Mackintosh' coats were produced in the 1820s. Charles set up his own company to produce the material in 1840.

Women's clothes

The basic style for women's clothes had been set before Victorian times. Women of all classes wore long dresses or skirts but the shape of these garments changed a lot throughout the era.

Shaping up

At the start of the Victorian age dresses had a more natural, flowing look. Gradually, over the years, more petticoats were added under the skirts and the skirts were pulled tightly into the waist, too. By the 1840s, dresses had a bell-shaped appearance. Then, in the 1850s the crinoline arrived. The crinoline was a sort of cage over which the skirt of the dress hung. It did away with the need for petticoats. However, getting through doorways or into waiting carriages was difficult for ladies in crinolines. Servants often copied their mistresses style of dress and were forever knocking things over with their large skirts.

↩ A lady is helped into her crinoline dress.

Written at the time

Nell Le Strange, the heroine of the Victorian novel *Cometh Up as a Flower* by Rhoda Broughton, published in 1867, talks about her inadequate dress:

'It [her dress] was ashamed of itself, I think, for it clung to me, limp and flabby, like a wet bathing-dress; and to complete my discomfiture, I discovered that my hair was dressed in a fashion that had died the death at least a year and half ago ... Several people (men especially) looked at me, and I attributed their notice solely to my outlandish attire.'

A touch of class

In Victorian times, clothes said more about a person's class than they do today. The well-off could afford fine fabrics such as silk and velvet. The boom in industry meant there were more middle class people. They could also afford decent clothing but tended to pick ready-made clothes. Poorer people often made do with second-hand or hand-made clothes.

Women of all classes were expected to cover up. Showing too much flesh was considered bad taste. Only ladies from the middle and upper classes could get away with baring any skin. Their evening dresses were often cut to reveal shoulders.

⬆ The latest fashions in an edition of the *Englishwoman's Domestic Magazine* from 1868. It shows women wearing dresses with frills and added decoration.

Ladies and maids

A Victorian lady changed her outfit a few times every day. Only the rich could afford to change their clothes to suit every occasion. Each time a lady's maid helped her to get dressed.

The lady's maid

A girl from a working class background was doing well if she became a lady's maid. She was responsible for looking after and repairing her mistress' clothes. She helped the lady in and out of her many layers of clothing as well as helping to dress her hair.

One of the perks of her job was often being able to wear her mistress' old clothes. Other maids and servants wore a kind of uniform. By the end of the Victorian era they wore a light cotton dress with a printed design in the morning when they did most of the heavy duty jobs. In the afternoon, they changed into black outfits with white aprons.

The metal frame that supported the bustle looked like a small cage.

A day in the life of...

...the Duchess of Marlborough who describes the outfits worn during a hunting party:

'To begin with, even breakfast ... demanded an elegant costume of velvet or silk ... We next changed into tweeds to join the guns for lunch ... An elaborate tea gown was donned for tea ... for dinner ... we adorned ourselves in satin, or brocade, with a great display of jewels ... That meant sixteen dresses for four days.'

Fashion in Photographs 1880 –1900, by Sarah Levitt, published by B.T Batsford in 1991.

Hustle and bustle

By the early 1870s lady's maids were helping their mistresses into the latest fashion – the bustle. People laughed at the crinoline but the bustle met with the same sort of criticism and laughter. It stuck out at the back of the skirt and was usually created using a frame. Sometimes, women used cushions stuffed with horsehair or newspaper to create the look. By the mid-1870s the bustle was already out of fashion.

Victorian magazines and newspapers often poked fun at the bustle.

Rebellion!

By the 1880s women were **rebelling** against clothes that covered them up. They wore shorter skirts, stopped wearing **corsets** and a few even wore **knickerbockers** – the first sort of trousers for women. Upper class women were more active and wore sporting costumes such as bicycling outfits and tennis dresses.

A Victorian lady shows off her bicycling costume. The 'leg-o'mutton' sleeves got their name because they were shaped like a sheep's leg.

Menswear

Clothes for men did not change much during Queen Victoria's reign and fashions remained quite formal throughout. It was not until the end of the era that men began to experiment.

⬆ The Victorian Prime Minister, William Gladstone, gave his name to a popular Victorian stiff white collar called a Gladstone collar.

The basic look

When Queen Victoria was born some men were still wearing **knee breeches**. But by the 1820s full-length trousers were fashionable. However, male servants often still wore knee breeches so that they looked different from their masters.

In the early Victorian days **dress coats** were also fashionable. These full-length coats were worn well past the knee. By the 1840s dress coats were worn mostly at night. During the day men wore **frock coats** to the knee. By modern tastes, the colours worn by men were plain. Dark blues, greens and black were the most popular and would remain so for most of the era.

Clothes make the man

In Victorian times people were aware of their place in society. The cut of the clothes and the kind of material worn said a lot about a person's wealth and class. Upper class men wore trousers often made from cotton or wool. Workers, farmers and servants wore rougher fabrics. **Corduroy** was considered fabric for working men because it was hard-wearing. Shirts were made from cotton, silk and linen. Fine linen shirts were considered the best quality. The very fact that they were difficult to clean and keep looking at their best was a sign that you were wealthy.

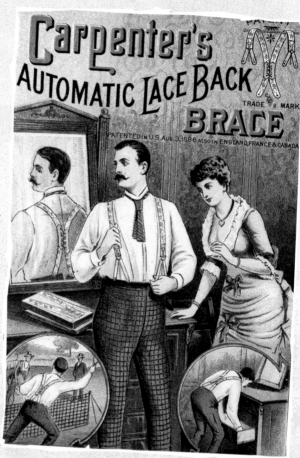

This advertisement from about 1880 shows a man sporting braces. Note that his trousers do not have belt loops. This is because wearing belts didn't become popular until the 1890s.

Suits you

The first suits with matching jacket, waistcoat and trousers were called 'lounge suits'. They were worn for sport and leisure and first appeared in the 1860s. However, it was not until the end of the era that men began to experiment with styles and colours. The author Oscar Wilde wore bright-coloured waistcoats and velvet knee breeches. Sports such as hunting and cycling, inspired practical clothing such as shorter trousers.

Written at the time

A description of the gentleman Angel Clare, as he worked as a farmer in Thomas Hardy's *Tess of the D'Urbervilles*, published in 1891:

'Under his linen milking-pinner he wore a dark velveteen jacket, cord breeches and gaiters, and a starched white shirt. Without the milking-gear nobody could have guessed what he was. He might with equal probability have been an eccentric land-owner.'

Children's clothes

Clothes for upper and middle class children were not designed to play about in as they were made from stiff fabrics. Children were expected to be neat and tidy. Poor children often just had rags to wear and went barefoot.

Garments for girls

All girls were expected to be **modestly** dressed. Just like their mothers, they wore dresses with long sleeves and high necklines. However, young girls wore shorter skirts even into their teenage years. The skirts were stiffened with petticoats with long knickers showing. It was a big moment when a girl could finally wear a long skirt.

⬆ *Cherry Ripe* is a famous painting by J.E. Millais, from 1879. The little girl is wearing a mop cap which was popular with girls and maids.

Written at the time

Cassells Household Guide, circa 1880s from the article *Children's Dress (1) – Clothing for Infants*:

'We would advise the young mother to avoid needless display, even though able to afford it. All purchases should be made at a good shop, where the articles sold may be relied on. All ostentation is vulgar, besides which babies are sufficiently attractive to need little adornment; and there is more elegance in simplicity.'

Boys' wardrobes

In richer families it was usually the mother who chose the children's clothes. Little boys were often dressed in smocks. Young boys mostly wore suits with frilly shirts and had long hair. The look was quite feminine. Fashions for boys also included kilts and sailor suits.

High morals

It didn't matter to which class a child belonged, they were expected to obey adults. It was believed that 'children should be seen and not heard'. From a young age they were expected to behave at all times. Children were also taught good **morals**. These attitudes influenced the kinds of clothes worn by upper and middle class children.

Rag-bags and street urchins

Poor children made do with whatever they could find. Old adult clothes were cut to fit them and street children often had nothing but rags. Some children earned money as crossing sweepers. They would clean a pathway across a mucky road for rich people who wanted to protect their clothes.

⬇ Poor children often went barefoot. If they did have shoes they were usually full of holes.

Underwear

Victorian underwear was not only fashionable but practical too. Layers of petticoats or vests helped to keep the Victorians warm. Underwear was also easier to keep clean than heavy outer garments.

Women's lingerie

Underwear for women was divided into two groups. There were underlinens such as petticoats, **chemises**, drawers and **camisoles**. These were usually delicate but could be washed easily. There were also structural garments such as corsets and bustles. From the 1820s, corsets became essential for women and even young girls. They helped to give them the appearance of a tiny waist. Most early corsets were made from whalebone and stiff cotton. They were very uncomfortable to wear and many women fainted if they were pulled too tight.

An advertisement for electric corsets, from about 1892. The electric charge from the corset was supposed to be good for the circulation!

Written at the time

Etiquette and advice manuals – *The Lady's Dressing Room*, by Baroness Staffe, translated by Lady Colin Campbell and published in 1893:

'A virtuous woman has a repugnance to excessive luxury in her underclothing. She does not like too much lace or embroidery or ribbons and bows. She has them trimmed, of course, but with a certain sobriety which speaks in her favour ... She prefers comparatively simple under-linen, which there is no fear of washing, and which can be changed daily.'

What a bloomer

In the later Victorian era, some women did not like the way corsets stopped them moving about, so they rebelled against them. In 1851, an American woman called Amelia Bloomer began wearing cotton trousers instead. These were gathered at the ankle under a knee-length skirt. These trousers eventually took her name and were called bloomers. However, when she visited England many women were appalled at her showing her legs and the trend never caught on.

Underwear for men

At the start of the period most men wore hand-made cotton or wool tops and bottoms. By the end of the era much underwear was produced in factories. An all-in-one woollen piece from America, called a Union Suit, became popular because it was easy to care for and was warm as it covered you from wrist to ankle.

The Union Suit was warm and practical.

Hats off

Nearly everybody wore a hat in Victorian times. Styles of hats changed during the era and were influenced by hairstyles. Hat etiquette was vital and there were plenty of rules about wearing a hat.

Some hats were made to cover most of the face. Others suited fashionable hairstyles.

Women's hats

The fashion in lady's hats changed many times during Queen Victoria's reign. The shape of hats were often created to fit women's hairstyles. In the 1830s, women wore buns or top-knots so hats tended to be high. By the 1850s hairstyles were flatter with ringlets or plaits at the side. Hats became smaller and styles such as the pill-box hat became fashionable.

Top hats for all

The **top hat** was the most popular hat for all men throughout the Victorian era. Less formal hats included the cap and a kind of **bowler hat**.

Some top hats could be folded so they could be placed under the seat at the theatre.

Hair for men

In early Victorian times a man's hair would have been neat with little facial hair. By the 1850s long and short styles were popular. Oil was applied to keep the hair in place. Men began sporting all kinds of beards and moustaches. One style was called 'mutton chop whiskers'. These were long bushy sideburns that got thicker at the mouth.

Hat etiquette

Women could wear hats indoors and outdoors. However, men were supposed to lift or remove their hats at different times. When you were outside it was good manners to lift your hat for a stranger. If you met a friend, particularly a woman, then you were supposed to remove your hat. It was very bad manners to leave your hat on indoors.

Victorian ladies did not like to get suntanned. At the seaside they wore bonnets to shade their faces from the sun. Men could leave their top hats behind and wear less formal hats such as straw boaters.

Shoes and boots

Throughout Victorian times people tended to wear leather boots. At the beginning of the era footwear was usually hand-made. By the end of the period more shoes were made in factories using machines.

⬆ An advertisement for boots and shoes from about 1895.

Men in boots

Victorian men usually wore practical leather boots. Gentlemen needed solid footwear for hunting and horse-riding. Working men needed tough boots that protected their feet. Boots were also best for walking through the filthy Victorian streets. The first lace-up shoes appeared in the 1860s. Shoes were considered to be casual but by the late 1890s they were becoming fashionable. Young men wore **spats** over **patent leather** shoes or slip-on pumps.

Arthur Wellesley, 1769–1852

Arthur Wellesley, the 1st Duke of Wellington, was a famous soldier and politician. He asked his London shoemaker to make him a leather boot that fitted under the longer trousers that became fashionable at the beginning of the eighteenth century. They were practical for a soldier but the Duke also wore them everyday. The fashion for his boots caught on in the 1840s and they became known as wellingtons. By the 1850s the first rubber wellington boots were produced.

Women's feet

Women often wore leather ankle boots outside. They became popular because women were not supposed to show their ankles. Shoes worn indoors by well-off women were more like slippers. They were often made from delicate material such as satin or silk and beautifully decorated with beads and ribbons.

These silk dancing shoes belonged to Queen Victoria. Shoes worn by rich women were very delicate.

Down at heel

In the seventeenth century, poor people were often called 'down at heel'. This meant they couldn't afford to keep the heels on their shoes repaired. The same was true of working class people in Victorian times. Shoes were often handed down from one family member to the next until they fell apart. Children living in slums were often barefoot. Many adults and children wore wooden clogs because they were cheap and hard-wearing.

Farmers and factory workers sometimes wore clogs to protect their feet.

Shopping for clothes

Shopping changed a lot between 1837 and 1901. At first clothes were hand-made from cloth bought in a shop. When machines took over, clothes production became faster and more people bought clothes 'off the peg'.

Sew your own

In the early Victorian years getting a new outfit was a big moment. First of all the fabric, cotton and buttons had to be purchased from a small shop. Ordering fabric by mail order was also popular.

The fabric then had to be made up into the clothes at home. All sewing was done by hand, usually by a female member of the household. If you were from a wealthy family then a servant or dressmaker might have made your clothes. When you wanted a new hat you visited a **milliner**. If you needed new shoes you went to a shoemaker.

Clothes off the peg

However, factories began to mass-produce clothes more quickly and cheaply. This changed the way people got their clothes.

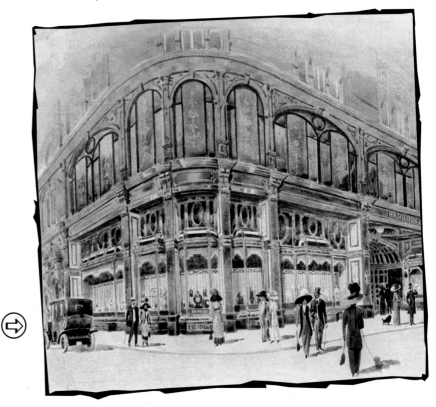

This old photograph shows one of London's most famous department stores, Harrods. You can still visit Harrods today.

By the end of the era people were enjoying the pastime of shopping. Large stores had opened in cities across Britain. Those who shopped at them were often wealthy upper and middle class people. Many of these stores sold clothes, household goods and even food. With special menswear, women's dress and children's clothes departments it meant the whole family could be kitted out in one place.

Down market

While the lower classes often worked in the factories that produced the clothes that went into these large stores, they could not afford to shop there. The poor continued to make their own clothes or shopped for second-hand clothes. In London the clothing market at Petticoat Lane was a good place to pick up a bargain.

The poor had to make do with second-hand clothes that kept them warm and protected them at work.

Charles Worth, 1826–1895

Charles Worth was an English dressmaker who was the first fashion designer. At thirteen he became an apprentice at a London fabric merchant. In 1846, he left England for Paris. By 1865 he was head of the House of Worth, the most famous design house in the world. His fabulous creations were individually made to fit each customer. Only the very rich could afford to buy his one-off pieces.

Timeline

1819	On 24th May Princess Victoria is born.
1820s	Mackintosh coats are manufactured for the first time.
1837	On 20th June Victoria becomes Queen of the United Kingdom.
1830s	Britain is the top cotton manufacturer in the world.
1840s	Tight-laced corsets to pull in the waist and make women appear more curvaceous become popular.
1846	Isaac Singer invents the Singer sewing machine.
1850s	The bell-shaped crinoline dress is fashionable.
1850	Prince Albert starts to wear a top hat, kick-starting a trend that lasts throughout the Victorian period.
1851	The Great Exhibition is held in Hyde Park, London from May to October.
1851	Amelia Bloomer wears cotton trousers, later called 'bloomers', rather than corsets for the first time.
1853–1856	The Crimean War takes place between Turkey and an alliance of Britain, France and Russia.
1858	Charles Worth opens the Worth design house in Paris, France.
1860s	The first suits, with matching trousers, jackets and waistcoats, are worn by men.
1861	On 14th December Prince Albert dies from typhoid fever.
1868	The all-in-one piece of underwear for men called the Union Suit is invented.
1870s	Dresses with bustles are fashionable until the mid-1870s.
1901	On 22nd January Queen Victoria dies, aged 81.

Glossary

acquired come to own

bowler hat a man's hard felt hat with a rounded top and small brim

British Empire countries overseas that belonged to Britain from the late seventeeth century to the middle of the twentieth century

camisole a sleeveless piece of female underwear that covers the upper body

chemise a loose-fitting piece of female underwear that hangs straight from the shoulders. It is worn under a corset

colony a territory overseas that is ruled over by another foreign power

corduroy a thick cotton fabric

corset a closely fitted piece of female underwear that is pulled tight to make the waist smaller

Crimean War the war between Russia, Britain and France against Turkey which lasted from 1853 to 1856

dress coat a man's jacket worn mostly in the evening

exhibit a public display of items

formal a set of rules

frock coat a man's coat with a long skirt that sweeps around the front and back

Industrial Revolution the name given to a time when steam-powered machinery was developed to do jobs previously done by hand

knee breeches close-fitting trousers that reach to or just below the knee

knickerbockers loose-fitting trousers that are gathered at the knee or calf

manufacturing making something with machines, usually in factories

military to do with soldiers and the armed forces

milliner someone who makes hats

modest describes a person who does not show off their achievements or parts of their body

morals standards of behaviour

patent leather leather with a shiny varnished surface

power loom a mechanised loom that was invented in 1784 by Edmund Cartwright

raw material the basic thing that is used to manufacture something

rebelling to fight against or resist something that is considered normal by most people

reign the number of years a King or Queen rules a country

spats cloth covers worn over shoes to protect them from mud and rain

top hat a tall felt hat with a flat crown and broad brim

treadle a lever that is moved by the foot, creating motion to operate a machine

Index

Resources

A *Victorian Childhood: At Home* Ruth Thomson, Franklin Watts 2007
Facts About: The Victorians Kay Woodward, Wayland 2007

www.bbc.co.uk/schools/victorians
An excellent website that summarises Victorian life.
www.victorianweb.org
Explore many different topics about the Victorians.